BORDER BUDDIES

Written by Melanie Lopata

Editor ~ Nay Merrill
Proofreader ~ Tina Sanders
Cover Illustrator ~ Denny Poliquit
Chapter 7 Photo Credit ~ Deborah Fast

Copyright © 2018
All rights reserved. This book or any portion thereof
may not be reproduced or used in any manner whatsoever
without the express written permission of the publisher except
for the use of brief quotations in a book review.

Printed in the United States of America

Luke and Cole are fun dogs and very smart. My husband and I adopted Luke when he was a puppy, just eight weeks old. A year and a half later, we rescued Cole from a bad home. Luke and Cole became brothers and best friends.

They love to play, take walks, run, and sometimes get into mischief. They know all of the doggy commands such as "sit" "stay" "shake" and more, and they know key words such as "treat" "ride" "car" "walk"! They also have a doggy brother named Hitch who is a Mountain Cur mix.

I love my dogs and cannot wait for you to join them on their first of many adventures in the fun series, *Border Buddies*.

CHAPTER 1

Luke and Cole were border collie dogs and they were different as night and day. As brothers, they stuck closely together, but their personalities were very different.

Luke loved to jump high to catch a frisbee, play in the snow, and snuggle with his owner to take a long nap.

Cole loved to chase tennis balls and small animals such as rabbits and squirrels, jump in mud puddles, and lie at his owner's feet to nap.

Despite their differences, they were always together and always got along.

One chilly October day, Luke and Cole were wandering around in their yard on the farm where they lived.

Cole was busy sniffing around for any signs of a squirrel that he could chase. He soon became bored and sat there staring at the woods.

"Luke, come on, let's go exploring in the woods. I'm bored," Cole said to his brother with a whiny sound in his voice.

Luke considered this for a minute. He didn't see what it would hurt to take a little hike and stretch their legs.

They could be back before supper.

Cole ran around excitedly. "Do you think our owners will mind?"

Luke rolled his bright, brown doggy eyes. His brother was so immature. Luke did what he wanted, not what his owners wanted.

"They won't even know we're gone," Luke replied. "Now hurry up. Let's go before it gets dark."

And without another word, Luke started towards the woods which sat near the farm property.

Cole skipped along behind Luke, loving the adventures that they went on.

He loved chasing the birds and squirrels and smelling trees and leaves.

They crawled under the fence and made their way to the wooded entrance, excited for their adventure.

After a few minutes of walking, both dogs were inside the woods. It was early afternoon, so it wasn't dark yet, but there were clouds over the sun which made it a little darker.

Cole skipped ahead of Luke, who usually lagged behind because he weighed more and was older. Sometimes he acted like an old man with his slow walking.

"Wait up, Cole," Luke called, panting heavily.

Cole slowed down, sniffing every tree along the way. He was familiar with these woods because their owners sometimes took them in to explore, but there were always new smells.

"Come on, we have to take this path," Luke called impatiently to his brother.

Cole caught up to Luke and they hurried down the path. Cole didn't know why Luke was in such a hurry all of the time.

Cole loved to explore and take his time, smelling everything new and old. And, of course, looking for squirrels to chase. Oh, how he loved to chase squirrels! It was a super fun game for him.

Luke, on the other hand, was way too focused on what he was doing to be bothered with squirrels.

A little further and the brothers found themselves standing next to a small river. Cole jumped into the water and even drank some of it.

"Luke, the water is great! Come on, it's not deep and we can cross to the other side," Cole called out as he jumped through the little river excitedly.

For someone who hates taking a bath, he sure is having fun in the water, Luke thought.

Luke didn't mind taking baths, but he was not about to walk through a river that could have gross fish and other things swimming around in it.

Luke decided to walk down next to the river and find a crossing spot, maybe with stones to step on.

Cole didn't realize that Luke walked away, and Luke didn't realize that Cole had not followed him.

A few minutes down the river, Luke looked behind him and didn't see Cole.

He turned himself around in a circle, hoping to see his brother somewhere. Cole was not in sight.

Luke became anxious and started heading back the way he came. When he got to the spot where he thought he left Cole, he saw that Cole wasn't there.

The sky seemed to be getting darker, which meant the sun was going down. He just had to find his brother!

In a panic now, Luke hurried back down the river bank and almost started to run, but he became out of breath.

He sat down next to a tree so he could rest and try to figure out where he was. Surely, he couldn't be lost.

He tried calling out to Cole by barking the way they usually did when they wanted to get each other's attention.

Luke heard nothing.

Oh man. I'm lost, and Cole is lost, and our owners are going to be so mad. And I'll miss dinner and my nice warm bed and there are probably mean animals out here, Luke thought anxiously.

Luke laid down next to the tree and closed his eyes. He thought maybe he could rest for a few minutes and catch his breath and calm down.

Suddenly, Luke felt a wet nose nudging at his face. He jumped up from his spot to see Cole standing in front of him, panting and smiling.

"Cole! Oh Cole, I thought I had lost you!" Luke cried out.

Cole excitedly jumped up and down and turned around in circles.

"Luke - you won't believe it, we have to cross this river!" Cole said with excitement. "I found a lot of holes where squirrels probably live and there are a lot of birds in the trees and lots of places to sniff."

Luke shook his head. "No, the sun is going down soon and we have to get back to the farm."

"Aw, you're no fun," Cole whined.

Luke led the way back to where he thought the farm was. He was anxious to get to his dinner and then have a nice biscuit treat. His owners always gave them biscuits after dinner.

Cole hurried after his brother, knowing he was right but disappointed because he wanted to explore the woods more.

CHAPTER 2

After walking for several minutes, Luke became anxious because he knew they weren't going in the right direction.

Cole romped happily beside Luke, not thinking anything of the way they were going. He always followed Luke and trusted him.

They came to a small opening in the trees and looked around. There was a lot of grass like a back yard would have, surrounded by trees.

Birds flew from tree to tree and the branches rustled around in the gentle breeze.

Cole ran into the opening to chase the birds. Luke stood at the edge of the clearing, wondering what to do next.

"This way, Luke!" Cole cried out as he ran to the other side. "Let's try this way!"

"That is not the way we came. We have to turn back into the woods, Cole. It's getting dark."

"No, this is the way, I can smell it. Come on!" Cole ran to the other side of the clearing where more trees stood.

Boy am I getting old, Luke thought as he ran after Cole. Luke could run pretty fast, but his hips bothered him once in a while.

When the boys reached the edge of the clearing, they went back into the woods. Darkness was falling fast and Luke had to squint to see his surroundings.

Cole was still up ahead and then suddenly he was out of sight! Luke ran in the direction he saw Cole run and stopped when he came to a steep hill. He looked down and saw Cole sitting at the bottom.

"Cole, are you hurt?" Luke yelled to his brother.

"No, I am fine. I slid down on my feet. But it is too steep to climb back up. You'll have to come down."

Luke glanced around the area where Cole was standing and saw nothing but darkness.

"No way, Cole. Hold on, you're coming up."

Luke looked around at the fallen tree branches, then searched through bushes and finally found a long sturdy branch.

He grabbed the branch with his teeth and dragged it to the top of the hill, then slowly let it down. When Cole latched on with his teeth, Luke pulled him up.

Thankfully, Cole wasn't hurt, and they could move on again.

"This way!" Cole walked quickly towards a path that lay in the woods.

Luke wasn't sure where that path came from, but he hurried to catch up with Cole.

They walked down the path, past fallen tree branches and large stones.

They came upon a small stream and drank from the water, then continued on. The birds were still chirping but as evening set in, the woods were quieter.

"Come on, we have to hurry," Luke panted as he began to walk away from the stream. He didn't want to get caught in the dark or miss supper.

Cole trotted along next to Luke as if he didn't have a care in the world. Well, he didn't! He was a carefree young pup who loved life and didn't worry about bedtimes or supper times or any time at all!

But Luke was older and set in his ways, so Cole usually followed along to please him.

After walking for what seemed to be hours, but really was only about fifteen minutes, Luke declared that they were lost. He suggested they find a spot near a tree and lie down and wait until their owners came looking for them.

Cole didn't like that idea. He had a lot of energy and wanted to run or walk more. But he did what Luke suggested to please him.

The boys found a large tree with a lot of leaves and branches to take shelter next to.

Luke curled up and closed his eyes to nap for a while. The sun was setting quickly now and darkness crept in.

Luke didn't like the dark. At home, he slept on his special dog bed and his owners always left a night light on for him. His owners were very special.

Cole couldn't close his eyes just yet, so he laid down but was on the lookout, his ears perking up every time he heard a sound. After a while, though, his eyes began to close. Boy was he sleepy.

CHAPTER 3

SNAP!

Luke and Cole's eyes flew open at the sound of a breaking twig nearby. They quickly sat up and looked around.

Luke's heart was beating very fast. He was afraid of what was lurking nearby. Cole wasn't afraid, though.

"Who's there?" Cole called out bravely.

"Hello? Just me, Sam," a nearby voice replied.

Luke and Cole couldn't see much, because it was very dark now, but the moon gave enough light through the trees that they could make out some shadows.

They watched as something moved slowly towards them. Cole huddled close to Luke. He was just a little afraid now.

"Hello there," the voice called out again. "I see you over by the tree. Coming your way. Don't be afraid."

After a minute, Luke and Cole could see the animal in front of them. Why, it was a fox!

He was smaller than Cole, but his head was held high as if he wasn't afraid of anything.

Cole stepped forward to greet the fox.

"Hello, my name is Cole. This is my brother, Luke. We are lost so we are sleeping here until morning or until our owners find us."

"Owners?" the fox asked.

"Oh, excuse me. My name is Sam. I'm not sure what 'owner' means. I run around the forest and provide food for my brothers and sisters and myself.

I was late tonight going home and happened to see you two lying here."

Sam sounded nice. Cole was excited now. They had a friend!

Luke was a little more cautious. He looked around anxiously, wondering where Sam's family was and if they were as friendly as Sam.

"My family is probably home sleeping now. I sense it's getting late. Sorry you two got lost. If you camp here for the night, I can show the way out of these woods in the morning."

"Oh, that would be very kind of you," Luke said, sitting back down.

"It's no problem at all. In fact, I can sleep next to this tree with you if you don't mind the company. Then we can leave early when the sun comes up."

The boys agreed to this and Sam settled down with them next to the tree.

The night was cool but without a breeze, so they were comfortable.

All around them, the boys could hear crickets, an occasional owl, and some other animal sounds that weren't too familiar to them.

Well, not familiar to Luke and Cole anyway. Sam knew the ways of the woods, most of the animals who lived there, and what went on day and night.

Sam and Cole stayed up late talking about Sam's adventures and family and friends.

Luke drifted off and surprisingly had a good night's sleep, even though he was sleeping on the hard ground and not in his soft bed at home.

CHAPTER 4

Luke was the first to wake the next morning because he hadn't stayed up all night talking like Cole and Sam had.

He stretched and looked around, remembering where they were and how they had gotten lost.

Cole and Sam were sprawled out next to the tree, snoring softly. Luke hated to wake them, but he had no choice. The sun had come up and it was time to find their way home.

"Cole, Sam, wake up," Luke called out.

Cole stretched and yawned, then curled up with his eyes remaining closed.

"COLE!" Luke barked out.

Cole slowly sat up. He was not a morning dog and didn't appreciate Luke waking him at this hour.

He didn't have to work on the farm today herding sheep, so why was Luke waking him up so early?

Sam stood up and looked like he was ready to go. He was always an early riser. There was too much to do in the day, such as hunting for food and making sure his home had enough bedding for sleeping.

Cole finally stretched and yawned a few more times, then he was ready to go. Luke rolled his eyes. He didn't like that his brother was so slow and took his time to do everything. They had to get moving if they wanted to make it home for breakfast!

The three friends set off in the direction that Sam pointed to and they walked for about ten minutes when Cole spotted a squirrel and began to chase it.

Luke and Sam ran after him, yelling for him to stop, but Cole kept running until the squirrel ran up a tree.

Cole stood at the bottom of the tree barking at the squirrel. The squirrel stuck his tongue out at Cole and scurried off.

Luke was panting heavily so he couldn't lecture his brother, but thankfully Sam did.

"Cole, we cannot run off!" Sam exclaimed. "We'll lose direction and you won't make it home by dark, if at all."

Cole put his head down and followed Sam and Luke back in the direction they started out from.

"So, tell me about this farm of yours," Sam said as they walked.

"Oh!" Luke exclaimed. "It's wonderful. There's a fence in the back of the farmhouse that goes for miles, with tons of grass and trees."

"Every morning after breakfast, we get let out of the house to help Farmer Bob let the sheep out to graze for the day," Luke continued. "Then we get to run around and explore for hours until lunch. After lunch, we take a nap."

"I don't take a long nap!" Cole exclaimed.

"No, you don't," Luke shook his head.

"Anyway, after our nap, we either go outside for the afternoon or head into town with our owner while he picks up supplies.

Sometimes when he is on his tractor, Cole likes to run along with it. Later, we herd the sheep into their pen for the night and then we have our supper and treats and lie down in the house with our owner and his wife before bed."

Luke loved thinking of the memories of their farm life. Oh, how he missed his home and longed to be there.

"Sounds lovely," Sam said. "Though I don't think I would want to be stuck in a fenced area all day or in a house. Foxes like to be free."

"You would love it!" Cole said happily as he trotted up next to Sam. "It's most wonderful. We are treated very well, bathed weekly, and never want for food. We don't even have to hunt for our food!"

"Yes, but I was born and raised in the woods. I don't think I would know what to do if I had to have an owner."

"You're right," Luke agreed. "You probably wouldn't."

After walking for about thirty minutes, the three decided to stop for water and a rest. Luke immediately fell asleep after lying down. After all, he usually had a nap after lunch.

Cole, however, had too much energy to lie down. He wanted to explore! He wasn't even concerned about getting home quickly. He just was happy to have some freedom for a while.

I bet I can do some exploring and get back before the other two wake up, Cole thought.

Cole peeked at Luke and Sam to make sure their eyes were closed and then slowly stood up and cautiously stepped away from the resting spot. When he was sure he wouldn't be seen, he began to run through the woods.

Cole ran back and forth between trees. He ran around trees. He ran and ran until he was very tired, and then decided to go back to the resting spot where Luke and Sam were napping.

But Cole was lost. He couldn't find the right direction to go, so he sat down wondering what to do.

Birds flew from tree to tree and squirrels jumped here and there looking for nuts on the ground.

Cole watched the squirrels in amusement, but part of him was frightened because he didn't know which direction to go in to find Luke and Sam.

Finally, Cole decided on a direction and began to walk. He walked past small streams of water, through thick brush, and along the trees, but still no sign of his brother and new friend.

He tried calling to them but heard nothing in response. What was he going to do?

In the meantime, Luke and Sam hurried along the path they had been walking for almost an hour and there was no sign of Cole.

"Cole!" Luke called out as loud as he could. "Cole, where are you?"

That stinker, Luke thought. *He always runs off and now he has gotten himself lost!*

Sam was ahead of Luke, walking as fast as he could and sniffing around every tree and bush to see if he could catch Cole's scent.

Luke started falling behind because he was tired and out of breath. *I have to get in shape,* Luke thought.

After walking around for a very long time, Luke and Sam finally came upon Cole, who was curled up at the foot of a tree with his eyes closed.

Luke ran over and put his paw on Cole to shake him awake.

Cole jumped up and ran around in circles because he was so excited to see his brother and friend!

"Now let's get serious and get you two back home," Sam said.

Luke and Cole followed Sam through the woods and back onto the trail. They were tired and hungry and happy to be headed home.

CHAPTER 5

The day was dragging on and Luke and Cole were still not home. They had no idea where they were, but they trusted Sam to get them out of the woods safely.

Luke lagged behind Sam and Cole because he was tired and his joints ached.

Suddenly, Luke's foot slipped into a small hole and he stumbled. Sam and Cole turned quickly when they heard Luke cry out.

"Luke! Are you hurt?" Cole cried out as he ran towards his brother.

Luke moaned in pain. "I think my foot is hurt."

Sam looked at Luke's foot and nudged it with his nose.

"Yes," he said shaking his head. "I think you sprained it. We can't keep walking. You need to stay off your foot for a while."

Luke wanted to cry. Not because of the pain, but because he just wanted to get home to his owners and curl up by the fireplace and take a nice nap.

He didn't want to be in the woods anymore. Why did he agree to go on an adventure?

"It's ok, Luke," Cole said softly. "It's going to be ok."

The three of them laid down for a while so Luke could rest his foot.

It was a quiet day in the woods and the air was getting cooler. It had to be late afternoon by now.

Hopefully the border collies would be home soon before it got dark.

Luke must have dozed off because he opened his eyes and Sam and Cole were not there!

He stood up in a panic and then remembered his hurt foot.

Quickly, he sat down and lifted his paw up. Not being able to balance that way, he ended up lying back down.

Luke let out a big sigh. He was tired of having a hurt paw, tired of these woods, and he was hungry.

Cole suddenly came bounding around a corner. Sam followed slowly behind.

"Luke, we may have found the path towards home!" Cole cried excitedly.

"Good," Luke grumbled. "I'm sick of this place."

The border buddies walked slowly behind Sam, and soon they came to a path that looked familiar. Cole was sure this was the path they started on when they began their adventure.

"I'm going to say good-bye here," Sam said sadly. "I've got to get home to my family. I hope you two will visit me someday."

Luke and Cole sadly said good-bye to Sam. It was always sad to leave friends behind but maybe someday their owners would take them on a nice hike in these woods and they could find Sam again.

The border buddies walked and walked...and walked. Luke had to rest several times because of his hurt paw. Cole was starting to yawn and the sun seemed to be fading.

Luke worried that they would have to spend another night in these woods. He didn't think his stomach could take the hunger, so he started to eat some of the grass next to the path.

"Luke," Cole said grumpily. "Dogs don't eat grass unless they're not feeling well. We aren't cows, you know!"

Luke rolled his eyes and kept eating. "I'm starving. I can't go on and this is all we have."

Cole hesitated and then started eating grass as well. It was better than starving, but boy did it taste gross. He didn't know how cows could eat this!

After their snack, the boys laid down for another rest. Just a short rest and they'd be on their way again.

CHAPTER 6

Cole opened his eyes suddenly and realized that him and Luke had fallen asleep! And they must have slept for a long time because now the sun was really fading and it was almost dark.

"Oh Luke," Cole cried. "We're going to have to spend another night here!"

"Come on," Luke urged as he stood up. "Let's walk as quickly on this path as we can. My paw feels better and I'm just going to have to deal with the pain so we can get home quickly."

The dogs hurried down the path with their heads down when the wind started to blow, and cold air hit their faces. Thank goodness it wasn't winter yet!

Finally, after a long time of walking, the border buddies happily realized they were near the clearing to their property and were almost home!

They began to run, even though Luke's paw still ached a little. He didn't care about the pain. He just wanted to get home.

They finally left the woods and entered their back yard.

They were so excited, they couldn't stop running until they reached the house.

Luke and Cole ran in circles by the door of the house and barked excitedly. Surely their owners would hear them and open the door.

But after several minutes of barking, they realized no one was coming out.

Cole walked around the side of the house, but as he looked at the windows, the house looked dark. He ran back to where Luke was waiting by the back porch.

"Luke, no one is home!" Cole cried.

"Check the driveway and see if the truck is there," Luke replied with panic in his voice.

Cole ran to the driveway. The truck was there. Where could their owners be if the truck was still there?

Luke suddenly stood up. He walked back towards the woods in a hurry.

"What are you doing?" Cole cried. "We can't go back in there! We'll get lost again."

"I bet our owners went to find us in the woods. We need to go back and find them, and we'll all walk back together."

Cole could tell that Luke wasn't about to change his mind, so he hurried after him.

Here we go again, Cole thought.

CHAPTER 7

Back in the woods, the border buddies stayed together this time and hurried along the path. They recognized the same sounds and trees and fallen branches. They came upon little streams of water that they hadn't seen earlier when they were here because they were in a hurry to leave.

Luke stopped to drink the water even though he thought it was gross. He liked the water in his dish at home, but he couldn't go thirsty in here, so he had to drink it.

Cole sat and waited while Luke drank. His ears perked up at every sound and his head moved back and forth as he watched leaves rustle around.

"Don't go running off," Luke called out.

No way was Cole going to run off again. He learned his lesson.

When Luke was done drinking, Cole took a quick drink and then they set off down the path again.

Suddenly, a large bird flew down at them and stopped on a log nearby.

Cole started to chase him, but the bird squawked loudly and Cole screeched to a stop.

"I'm here to help you," the bird said. "You must be looking for someone because there are two humans on the path ahead and they're calling for Luke and Cole. I am assuming you are Luke and Cole."

Luke was so relieved! He told the bird they were lost and the humans were their owners.

"I don't know the word 'owner,'" the bird said curiously. "But I can take you to the humans. Just follow me, and please do not go slow. I have things to do!"

The bird flew off ahead and Cole and Luke had to trot to keep up.

Up the path, around a corner, over a small stream, and onto a different path. Luke was tired again. He tried calling out for the bird to slow down, but the bird didn't hear him.

"Luke, hurry up!" Cole shouted. "We have to get to our owners."

Luke couldn't do it. It was too far and too fast. He let Cole run ahead and laid down on the path. Where in the world did Cole find his energy?

In the meantime, Cole had run ahead, not realizing that his brother had stayed behind. He followed the bird for about a mile, and suddenly, he heard voices. Human voices!

Cole barked loudly, determined for them to hear him. He then called out to thank the bird, who squawked in return and flew off.

"Cole! Here boy, come here!" a voice shouted.

Cole ran to the voice. Oh, how excited he was!

He came to a clearing and finally spotted Farmer Bob and his wife. He bolted over to them and jumped up, which was not normally allowed, and licked their faces.

Farmer Bob and his wife laughed and gave Cole hugs.

"Cole, where is Luke?" Farmer Bob asked suddenly. He looked around not seeing the other dog.

Cole barked and ran in a circle before bolting down the path to where Luke was.

"Wait up!" Farmer Bob called.

Cole tried to go slow so he wouldn't lose his owners.

After several minutes, he finally found Luke. When Luke spotted his brother, he stood up and stared anxiously, wondering if his owners were behind Cole.

Sure enough, Farmer Bob and his wife came into sight and Luke quickly walked towards them. He didn't dare run, as he was trying to rest his hurt paw as best as he could.

Farmer Bob and his wife gave Luke the same attention and affection they had given to Cole. Then, they gave the dogs a few biscuits to eat and some water from water bottles they carried.

Finally, Farmer Bob said they must hurry to get home.

Cole proudly led the way, while Luke stuck to his owners' sides, not daring to let them out of his sight. Finally, the clearing came where they knew they were home.

When Luke spotted the farm, he ran to the fence, not worrying about the pain in his paw. He crawled under the fence and anxiously waited for the pack to catch up. He couldn't believe he was home!

* * * * *

Later that evening, after a very big supper and several biscuits, the dogs laid in front of the fire in the living room while Farmer Bob and his wife petted them lovingly.

They were finally home, done with their adventure, and ready to wait awhile before they had another.

Visit this author's website at
www.melanielopata.weebly.com and
find her on Facebook at
www.facebook.com/MelaniesBooks

The author also owns an editing and
self-publishing consulting company called
Get It Write.
You can view her website at
www.getitwriteeditingco.com

www.ingramcontent.com/pod-product-compliance
Lightning Source LLC
Chambersburg PA
CBHW051412290426
44108CB00015B/2255